The Small Business Time Saver:

Tools To Automate Your Business Processes, Promote Yourself & Delight Your Customers Online

Andrew McCauley & Heather Porter

WE LIVE AND BREATHE THE MARKETING AUTOMATION MAZE AND WANT TO GIVE YOU OUR SHORTCUTS...

We have helped over 10,000 business owners worldwide use automation to remove themselves from doing the things they can't stand doing in their businesses.

When you are able to let go of the tasks that wear you down, you suddenly have a business you love (and one that makes you money on autopilot)!

Here is where to GO NOW to get our latest findings: aybguide.com

We share things like:

- How we have tripled our traffic to our website
- Our favorite email auto-responder scripts
- Free trial access to our Digital Traffic Institute online community

We welcome you to join a community of business owners fed up with being a slave to their business!

CONTENTS

Introduction   Pg i

1   Why Automate?   Pg 1

2   Who Should Automate?   Pg 4

3   The Interesting Thing about Extra Time   Pg 7

4   Website Content Planning, Creation & Promotion   Pg 9

5   Lead Generation And Follow-Up   Pg 21

6   Sales Tools   Pg 34

7   Customer Service Solutions   Pg 40

8   Tools To Manage Your Finances   Pg 47

9   Time Management & Task Simplification   Pg 51

10 Case Studies   Pg 57

    Get Our Marketing Automation Shortcuts   Pg 62

INTRODUCTION

Hi there and welcome to our book on business automation! We are excited to share great tips and tricks with you so that you can automate your business. All business owners who stop trading time for money, and learn to build a business and not a job, understand and use the principles of automation. Once you master them you will have more time for what matters most to you in life.

You may be wondering who exactly we are and why we know so much about this stuff so we'd like to give you a bit of an introduction first...

Heather Porter mastered scaleable systems when she promoted and managed events in over 25 countries for her own business and some of the world's most well-known speakers such as Tony Robbins. She learned the difference between successful entrepreneurs and those who struggle past start-up as Co-Founder of the Billionaire Adventure Club, an adventure travel club for entrepreneurs. In 2008 she shifted gears to help her clients target their global followings by building membership sites, teaching online marketing and helping to build online systems. She now focuses her time as one of the Co-Founders of automation agency Autopilot Your Business, while consulting and speaking.

Andrew McCauley is the other co-founder of Autopilot Your Business. He worked in hospitality for 17 years where he mastered marketing. In 2006, he started a business consulting company. During this time he traveled the world teaching business owners how to implement and use Social Media and Online Marketing for their own companies. While running his business he also ran the staff for seminars for 3 very large personal development companies across 8 countries and was a trainer and Director of Coaching for T Harv Ekers' Ultimate Internet Bootcamp. He now focuses on running his digital agency and regularly speaks. In 2015, Andrew was voted in the Top 100 Most Influential People on Twitter

We have helped many business owners get out of overwhelm, be more profitable and have more free time and are going to share what we know here so that by the end of this book, you will have a good idea of the tools which will allow you to automate many parts of your business! Some of the tools we share will completely automate a process, while others will not entirely automate, but will simplify it so that you get through it more quickly. Whatever stage you are at now, we hope you will find at least one thing that you can implement to make life in your business a little easier…

1. WHY AUTOMATE?

Funnily enough, despite the advances in technology going on all around us, many people today are busier than ever before. There is no accident as to why we called our business "Autopilot" Your Business!

At a recent engagement speaking to a group of business mentors, mostly made up of former CEOs and senior businesspeople, Andrew was approached by the curriculum manager of the program. "You know what? Our mentors need to know this. Can you come back and do a workshop for them?" It turned out that while most people there had heard a little bit about automating business, they really had no idea how to go about it until that talk.

That seems to be a recurring theme; while people have heard that there are great tools available to help them automate their business processes, they are often so busy or out of touch or intimidated by technology that they have not investigated further how automation could work for them. Or they sometimes don't even know what they can automate or think it means hiring more staff or spending a lot of money. However, because of the rise of start-ups and small businesses there is also a rise of tools available to them to support their business processes.

Let's have a look at what's currently going on: a recent survey by research firm Software Advice revealed that nearly all small-business software buyers are shopping for marketing-automation software for the first time. On top of that, 47% are still using manual methods to manage their marketing, while we already know an even larger percentage are still using manual systems for tasks such as invoicing and customer service. This represents hours of wasted time that could be better spent on growth activities for the business, or even more personal time for the owners.

This is one of the main benefits of automation; the ability to leverage time. After all, if you decided to pursue a dream and start your own business, you didn't swap a 40 hours per week job for the desire to work 70 hours a week in your business, did you? Automation will help you get out of that cycle, reclaim time and spend more of it working 'on' rather than 'in' your business.

What we're really talking about is systemizing. Think about all of those things that you do in your business repeatedly - these are the things you want to target for automation. For example, do you repeat certain training to staff over and over? Or perhaps you keep answering the same questions for clients? These are the things that need to be documented and automated. Systemizing in this way allows you to reach more people in less time. Bear this in mind as you go through this book; take notes so that you can go back and put systems in place for your business.

We've all heard the term 'work smarter, not harder' – this book is all about hooking up the "smarter" part. The key is to have the right tools and systems in place so that your business is automated or at least as simplified as possible.

We will be sharing some of our favorites with you as we go through this book.

Our last reason why you should automate is quite simply to minimize or eliminate human error and therefore keep costs down. Here's an example for you that will resonate with many business owners; how do you go about organizing your accounting?

Say you enter all of your transactions manually into an Excel spreadsheet (and many still do!), then pass that spreadsheet onto your accountant for end of year tax time. Your accountant finds that some of the numbers don't quite add up and needs to go through and fix up your books. Now, not only have you spent a lot of time with your Excel sheet, you will now pay more to your accountant for the extra time taken to get your accounts in order!

As we mentioned earlier, do you have certain processes that you or others in your team always need to train staff in? If you don't have a documented system, it could result in a 'Chinese whispers' effect where not all information is passed on, or it is passed on inaccurately.

These are just a couple of examples of how automation can help prevent human error. In the end, preventing error will save time and money that would have been spent on fixing mistakes!

2. WHO SHOULD AUTOMATE?

Who should automate? Well, we think anyone in business should look at what they can potentially automate to free up more time, but let's look at some specific examples. As we go through them, make a note to yourself – do you do the particular activity we are talking about? If so, note this down as something you can go back to later to consider automating

Client Management

First up, do you keep a spreadsheet list of client details or a box of client or contact cards somewhere? If yes, note down that you are a candidate for automation!

Lead Generation

How do you generate new prospects and leads? If you still do a lot of door-knocking and "cold" approaches and don't have any systems set up to bring them in automatically, then automating your lead generation should go down on your list!

Email

When it comes to emailing clients, do you manually send out emails to your client list? Or, worse, do you not send out emails to your client list at all? If this is you, note this down!

Accepting Payments

Next up, how do you take payments for your business? Is it always either over the phone or in person? If so, this means a person always has to be present in order to accept payments. Wouldn't it be great if payments just came in and you didn't have to be involved? Imagine waking up in the morning and finding that your business is making money as you sleep…That's right, if this is you then note this down for automation!

Invoicing

Along with how you take payments, how does invoicing work for your business? If you are manually sending out invoices and chasing up payments, consider adding this to your automation list!

Customer Feedback

Here's one that people often overlook; how do customers give you feedback? If you have to actually approach customers and ask for feedback, this impacts on your time. If you don't have an automated system in place, you will often find that the only voluntary feedback you get is when something has gone wrong. We can show you some great tools for automating customer feedback so if this sounds like you, add this to the list!

Social Media

Ok, here's one that many are guilty of outside of the business context; but do you end up spending far too much time on social media in relation to your business? Or, do you find yourself spending a lot of time looking at the latest videos and "Grumpy Cat" memes when you thought you would just quickly create posts for your business? Again, there are some great tools to help you automate much of your social media; we will show you some of these further on.

Accounting

Do you keep a shoebox or filing cabinet somewhere full of receipts? If you have any kind of manual system for your accounting, there is something out there for you that will help you to take back your time.

Quotes & Proposals

Another great one is proposal writing – do you spend a lot of time writing proposals for people? There are some brilliant automated proposal systems that can even track the proposal and what the potential client is looking at. We'll talk a bit more on these tools later on too!

Data

Lastly (although we could use other examples!), do you spend time entering some kind of data manually, whether that is accounting or other data? If so, automation could be a real time-saver for you!

Did you recognize yourself or your business in one or more of these examples? If so, make sure you have noted them down so that you can start developing your plan to automate!

3. THE INTERESTING THING ABOUT EXTRA TIME…

Now that you are looking at which of your activities could possibly be automated, have you thought about what you will do with the extra time you are freeing up? This is an exercise we do at speaking engagements with some interesting results...

So first of all, imagine you have two extra hours per week up your sleeve; what will you do with them? How will you spend the time? An example of what we are doing, now that more and more of our processes are automated, is taking a whole day to look at content creation. This means we record a podcast, create written content such as blog posts, and post comments to other blogs. This is a very important activity for our business; being online means that we need to ensure that we keep our content fresh and that our business is well-positioned in all the right places.

Alright, what if you had an extra five hours per week freed up? That's an extra hour for every weekday that you could be working on something important. Here are some of our suggestions; take your most important (or five most important) clients out for a coffee, work on something new for your business (such as a new product or service) or take the time to learn something new. So many people would like to be able to learn something but lack the time to do so, five extra hours is a lot of learning time! Don't forget, what you do doesn't have to be work-related; you could also take personal time for yourself and take a yoga course, a painting class or whatever it is that you have wanted to do for yourself.

Now, here's where it gets interesting; ten hours per week! When we have spoken to seminar audiences through this exercise, the comment that frequently comes back is that many simply can't comprehend actually having an extra 10 hours per week so do not know what they'd do with it! Ten hours is a lot of time to an entrepreneur, imagine what you could achieve with it! Many people seem to just fill up their day – no matter how much time they have they will fill it up with stuff; so if you really think about it productively, what could you get done with this extra time?

The key thing here is to think about all that stuff that you do repeatedly, day in and day out and picture what you could get done if all of this was automated. Many people are so busy spinning their wheels, getting those daily activities done that they can't even fathom having extra time available and haven't really thought about what they could achieve with it. When you start to learn about the tools we are going to teach you, it is an eye-opener as you realize that they are often easier than you may think...

4. WEBSITE CONTENT PLANNING, CREATION & PROMOTION

If you've spent any time in the last few years investigating or implementing online marketing strategies, you probably haven't missed the importance of creating quality, unique content for delivering value to your audience and driving traffic to your website.

The thing is, everyone *knows* they should be delivering good content, but many still run up against a brick wall in terms of time to create, ideas of what to create and how to promote that content for best effect. In this chapter we have some tools that can help to streamline the process…

WEBSITES

First up, we want to give you an overview of websites, platforms they are built on and why you can begin to automate some of that content.

Nearly everyone we work with is using a website platform called WordPress to build their websites. We love this platform as it is very easy for people to use and has a lot of functionality you can put with it. Basically, if you can operate a Microsoft Word program, you will pick up WordPress fairly easily. It allows you to easily create blog posts and update your website yourself, without needing an expensive webmaster or to wait until your webmaster has time for your updates to be done.

Plus you have the ability to schedule your blog posts. This means you can sit down whenever you have the time and write a few at once, then schedule them to publish throughout the month.

Why is this important? Basically because if you have a good website with quality content that is going up consistently, you will find that your website is more easily found in Google searches and you will have great info to share in your emails to your prospects and on social media. This regular traffic going back to your website will not only help with your Google rankings, but also keep you front of mind as an up-and-coming brand.

The important thing about being able to automate your blog posts is that it can provide you with some relief in terms of time pressure. There is a lot of debate about how often you should post new content to your blog and we find that people often panic at the idea that they should be blogging daily or even a couple of times a week. If you look at it from the point of view that you are able to automate the posts, you really only have to set aside one or two days per month to get into your creative head-space, sit down, and write. The scheduling function means that you then don't have to worry for the rest of the month.

Think of it like this; businesses that are successful on the internet tend to be those who use publishing and content creation as part of their marketing strategy. Those that are the most successful create quality, original content and post that content regularly. They also utilize a content calendar for strategic planning, and set aside some time to plan, create and promote content.

The important thing is how you look at it - see it not as something overwhelming but as a task that is simple and easy to accomplish if you put a system in place and set aside the time. If you divide the activities which make up a successful content strategy into chunks and use some of the tools available to make the task easier, it all starts to seem much more manageable…

TOOLS TO HELP PLAN AND CREATE CONTENT

While these tools won't *automate* your content, if a big part of your process involves staring off into space, trying to come up with content ideas, these will help you to make educated choices for what you run with and keep you on-track with where each piece is at. After all, it's always easier to follow a plan than to come up with stuff on the fly, right?

While content strategy and marketing is a topic for another book, a key part of nailing content is to start by identifying who your targeted audience is and what the end-purpose is for the piece of content. We would start by outlining a few topic "buckets" that fit in with your goals, then use these tools to help…

Buzzsumo

One great strategy that will simplify your content creation process is to identify popular pieces of content on your topic and look to better them. Buzzsumo is an excellent tool for helping with this; simply type in your topic or keywords and it will pull up popular content from the search period you choose. You will see the number of social shares as well as who shared it, giving you the added opportunity to reach out to those sharers with your new piece of content later.

Trello

A content calendar will help you to keep your ideas organized and make sure that you stay on track with a regular schedule. Trello has many possible uses (including creating to-do lists), but its simple format is also great for keeping an up-to-date content calendar. We create one "card" per piece of content, use the back of the card for notes, lists or related links and move it between lists on our content calendar "board" so that we know exactly what part of the process each piece is in.

The "lists" we use on our content calendar board look something like this:

Content Ideas	Researching	On Hold	Writing	Pre-Publish Check	Promotion	Schedule Review

All content ideas initially go into the first list, then are moved around from there. As Trello allows you to add due dates and various other features, it makes it easy to put in publishing and review dates too. You could think of it as a replacement for your whiteboard, only with room for more information to be stored.

Edit Flow

This is a free WordPress plugin which will allow you to create and manage your content calendar, all within your WordPress dashboard. You can see what you have planned out at a glance and move items around with a simple drag and drop interface. Edit Flow will sync with iCal or Google Calendar if you want to view it outside of WordPress, and allows for assigning to and reporting for team members if you have multiple people creating your content.

Kifi

How many times have you come across a great piece of content online that you think you may refer to later, but then can't find it on your reader or in your bookmarks without an extensive search? Kifi is a tool which replaces the need to use bookmarks (saving your hard drive space!), by allowing you to create topic-based "libraries" to save web content to. You can share your libraries with others or keep them private, and add tags of your choosing to content which you can use to search by later – easy!

Google Docs

There are a few things that make Google Docs a good choice for streamlining your content creation process:

1. It's free!
2. You can use it for distraction-free writing and research. If you select 'research' from the 'tools' drop-down, a search box which uses Google search will open to the right of your document so that you have everything in one screen.
3. You save your documents into the Google Drive cloud, which means that you can access them off any device and from anywhere with an internet connection.

Wordy

We know you tend to put a lot of time and effort into your digital products or opt-ins, so it's worth taking care that your reputation is upheld by ensuring that it is professionally edited. Wordy is a stand out because work is completed literally within minutes of you requesting it. You choose your payment level for your account – each bracket will give you a certain number of edited words and pages. There is no subscription so once your allocation is used up, you just need to top up your account if it's something which you will continue to use.

Elance, Zerys, Media Bistro, Rachel's List, Scripted, WriterAccess, Contently...

... yes there are a HUGE number of options out there! If you need to remove yourself from the content creation picture altogether, these are all sites on which you can find qualified freelancers to do the task for you. We suggest that you check for references and work samples as part of your hiring process, and perhaps initiate a trial period to see whether the freelancer "gets" your brand voice.

Of course one of the great things about hiring freelancers is that you can find some very talented people, but you eliminate the usual personnel and cost aspects of employment. The usual rules tend to apply in terms of "getting what you pay for" though; if you want really high-quality work, expect to pay a bit more to get someone with experience...

TOOLS TO HELP PROMOTE YOUR CONTENT

Website content is not a case of "create it and they will come", not unless you're Seth Godin or another expert who is well-known and sought-after in their field. That means the average business owner who creates a new piece of content needs to put some time into promoting it through various channels.

A rule of thumb that has been discussed among content marketing experts is that you should put at least as much time into content promotion as you did into creating the piece of content. There's no sense in investing time and money into creating content if it doesn't get seen!

There are a number of avenues you can go down, but if you want to create more time for yourself and a consistent experience for your business, then you need to create a system for what you do. These tools will help with your content promotion:

Process St

Process St allows you to create checklists for all the different steps that you take through a process. While you can use it for any process which you repeat in your business, we find it particularly helpful for content promotion and tracking where each piece of content is within the process.

With this tool you can create templates that are able to be duplicated – so what we do is repeat the template for each new piece of content so that we know a consistent process is being followed.

Process St is a free tool and allows you to give team members access. This means you can assign tasks and everyone is kept in the loop as each person checks off the items they are responsible for.

Snip.ly

For all of those times that you share someone else's piece of content on your social media sites, wouldn't it be great if people could somehow come back to yours? Snip.ly solves this by allowing you to create a banner that will display on the webpage that you share.

You get to choose the settings for any banner, including where on the page it displays, the call to action and button, color and link which you want to direct people to. They have even made it easy by creating a browser extension which will automatically pop up when you share a website URL.

Outbrain

This is a paid service which puts your content into "related content" or "popular on the web" spots on other, highly-trafficked websites. Prices start at $10 per day, but for that your content can be featured on prominent sites such as CNN or Slate.

The advantage of using this kind of paid platform is that your content can potentially reach a far wider audience than what you are able to through social media platforms, as their aim is to serve your content to people who are already actively looking in your topic area. This means that the traffic you get is potentially a warmer audience than those you might find via Facebook advertising.

Shareaholic

A great way to have ongoing promotion for your content is to ensure that others can easily share it and that your old content shows up as "recommended" or "related" content along with your new pieces.

Shareaholic is a free tool that will do these things automatically for you. Features for your website include social share buttons, social follow buttons, a 'recommendation engine' and analytics. If you want a different way to earn some money, you can even choose to include selected promoted content with the recommendations.

Influencers

Having an influencer in your field share your content is a powerful marketing tool. How can you get this to happen? Here are a few ways to help:

- **Buzzsumo** – We mentioned this tool before, but once you have created your content you can use Buzzsumo to identify people who have previously shared similar content and reach out to them. Also ensure that you mention influencers with popular content in the piece you produce and tag them in your relevant Twitter posts, this way you can reach out to them too.

  If that all sounds like a lot of work, this is actually a task that a good VA can do. Get them to compile a list of influencers and send them an email based on a template you create. Give them some guidelines so that an individual touch is added to each email, this way you don't come off sounding robotic.

- **Klout** – This tool scores social media user's influence on a 100 point scale – 50 or higher means that they are very active and you will find top influencers at closer to 100. Klout makes it easy to find who the main influencers are for a given topic, all you need to do is type in the topic in the search box and top influencers will be displayed on the right hand side of the page.

At the very least, following the highest rated people in your field will give you ideas, but you could also try to develop a relationship with them on social media – try following them and regularly joining in any conversations. It is possible with persistence, to get yourself known well enough that a reach-out just may get a response…

- **Exposely** – This "pay to play" option connects brands with influencers who will share their content. Campaigns start at $100 so you do need to have some marketing budget for this platform. The advantage of connecting this way is that you don't need to go to the trouble of identifying and contacting influencers yourself.

SOCIAL MEDIA

Part of your content promotion strategy should always involve the social media platforms which you already use. If you are concerned with finding the time to update all of your social media accounts on a daily basis, there are some great solutions available for you to set up and automate posts for sharing your content and for your other updates. We will look at these in this next section.

We don't recommend that you automate the entirety of your social media, as you could find yourself losing engagement without the 'human touch'. There is also evidence to show that Facebook gives preference to posts which you have created directly on their platform (it's in their interests to have you there as they can present you with advertising). Other social media platforms could easily follow this example, so we recommend you strike a balance between automating posts and posting directly on the social site.

Whichever way you share your posts, make sure you actively monitor and respond to any comments, or even thank people for sharing. The point of social media is that it's "social", if you don't engage then neither will your audience. For this reason we recommend that you never just "set and forget" with any social media tools!

Hootsuite

Hootsuite is a dashboard that links to most of the common social media accounts, including Facebook, Twitter, LinkedIn, Google Plus, Instagram, Tumblr and YouTube. Basically, instead of you having to log in and out of each account individually to make updates, you can update the whole lot from your Hootsuite account.

Scheduling is a fantastic feature of Hootsuite. You can go in and set up a series of posts to go to any of your social media accounts and you can even set those for specific days and times. You will also be able to see how people respond to your posts and interact with anyone who comments or sends you a message through your Hootsuite account.

A feature we particularly love is their bulk uploader for Twitter messages. You can create a formatted spreadsheet of tweets, dates and times and upload this directly to Hootsuite for scheduling. This saves you a bunch of time!

For anyone who has ever thought "I'll just quickly go in and update Facebook" then ended up spending far more time than you intended reading all the other posts on there, then Hootsuite is a great solution for saving you time and removing the temptation to linger for too long in social media accounts. This is good news for your productivity; Hootsuite doesn't show you all of the extra bells and whistles that you will see logging into your social media accounts, so you will only see what is really necessary for you to see on your own accounts. If you want to spend more time checking out what's going on in social media, you can schedule time outside of your allotted work time and not worry about that being eaten into.

Another great feature of Hootsuite is that they have an applet available for your internet browser. For example, if you use Chrome or Firefox you can install the applet into your tool bar, then when you are surfing the web and find an interesting article, photo or post you can click on the applet button and add your own comment, "check this out" etc. From there it will shrink the URL (website address) for you and you can schedule it as an upcoming post.

What we have found is that many people will comment "I don't know how to measure my ROI for social media". This tends to be because people get caught down a wormhole with it and are mixing business and personal time on their social media accounts. You can change this by using a program such as Hootsuite every time you want to update social media for business. It's great for being able to check out your stats and engagement results without going off-track into the latest funny video or whatever else has been posted.

Hootsuite is free for up to three social media accounts and after that you would need to upgrade to the premium version which allows you to have all of your accounts on there starting from $9.99 per month. This also gives you more advanced analytics and the ability to add team members to your account.

You can also run Hootsuite from your mobile phone using either their iPhone or Android apps. This means that if you are on the move and have downtime, such as while waiting for appointments, you can use that time to update your social media accounts. Check out their online tutorials if you would like to learn more about what you can do and how to do it.

Buffer

Like Hootsuite, Buffer allows you to schedule social media posts across different platforms from one dashboard. You can monitor analytics and respond to engagements all in the one place.

Buffer also offers a browser extension which makes it easy to schedule posts on the go. Unlike Hootsuite, there is no bulk uploader option for tweets, however Buffer has its own unique features which will appeal to some – it's just a matter of preference. For example, with Buffer you can select different preferred posting times for each of your social media platforms in your account settings. This means that you can schedule once across different channels without having to change the times.

Other Tips For Social Media Posts

Creation of posts and images to promote your content on your various social accounts is a simple task which you may like to outsource or hand to another team member. While we create most of our other social media posts ourselves, we get a team member to come up with 5 different social media posts and images per platform for each piece of content we create.

We also get a team member to pull out around 20 tweetable "snippets" from each blog post. They can put these straight into a spreadsheet that is formatted for the Hootsuite bulk uploader. These are uploaded into Dropbox where we can easily find them. A great time saver!

MONITORING SOCIAL MEDIA

While Hootsuite and Buffer will allow you to monitor any @ mentions of your Twitter handle, or mentions where you have been tagged, you will not see where your name and business has been mentioned if you were not tagged.

It is important that you know when you are mentioned, or when a topic is discussed publically that is close to your business, as that will give you the opportunity to respond or join in. There are some other tools which will help you to monitor brand mentions and even mentions of keywords of your choosing across the web. Here are some to explore:

Mention

Mention is a software platform that monitors across social media platforms, websites, blogs, forums and any other page on the web. It allows you to respond immediately by connecting your social accounts to their platform, and provides a robust analytics program. They will also email you with your alerts. You can have one alert set up for free, after that you need to go onto one of their subscription plans.

Social Mention

This is a free service which helps you to see brand mentions and interactions in a simple visual format. You will also see a rating of your brand's strength and whether it is viewed in a positive, negative or neutral light. Unlike Mention, you can't link your social accounts or receive email reports, but you can get an RSS feed for your preferred keywords for easy monitoring.

Talkwalker

Talkwalker is also a free service and monitors mentions across social media. You can learn about engagement, influencers, geographic data and other metrics such as sentiment analysis. If you wish, Talkwalker will also allow you to grab historic data that is up to two years old.

WEBINARS

Webinars are a great way of leveraging your time by being able to record your content once, then offer a replay. You could use video and audio, or go with an option that is just audio.

Here are some programs to check out, as with anything, you might want to try their free trials to decide what you like best:

- **GoToMeeting** – This has been around for a while and is a paid subscription service. While it is one of the pricier options, it has the ability to integrate with many different accounting and sales solutions too.
- **Instant Teleseminar** – An easy platform to use for primarily audio calls, but you can also preload and show a slide show online. Plans start at $47/month.

- **Webinar Jam** – This solution uses Google Hangouts and allows unlimited attendees (most other solutions have prices that are tiered with attendee numbers). It is cheaper at $297 per year and allows features such as registration, reporting, chatroom and polls or surveys (amongst many others). A downside is that by working with Google Hangouts, it can experience issues where Hangouts aren't working or delays of 20-40 seconds to what you are saying in real time.

- **DIY Method** – If you don't need too many fancy features and are on a low budget, then you can always set up a live Google Hangout, embed it onto a webpage and use Chatroll embedded on the page to allow viewers to ask questions. Chatroll allows a free account for lower numbers of participants (so you will need a paid account for larger numbers). We have used this many times, usually quite effectively, however we experience occasional issues with Google Hangouts being delayed as compared to the Chatroll, or interruptions to the coverage of the hangout.

SURVEYS

Surveys can not only be a great source of market research, but an excellent basis for creating new content based on your results. You could choose to set up one question or a basic poll on your website or in a newsletter, or you could go for a more comprehensive multi-question survey. We love **Survey Monkey** for providing free online-based survey software, but you could also try a paid version such as **SurveyGizmo** for more advanced requirements.

5. LEAD GENERATION AND FOLLOW-UP

When you automate your lead generation and follow-up you will be amazed at how much easier it is to turn prospects into customers. You can measure your results and create a budget to fund your growth. . In the last chapter we talked about the importance of good content for improving your

Google search results, attracting more visitors to your site and sharing good content with your current fans to keep your brand front of mind; the next thing that is vital for your online survival is what you do with those visitors once they have gone into your site.

You need to be able to capture those visitors as soon as they enter your site because the chances of them returning again are close to 1%. Plus of those who are interested in your products or services 80% won't buy the first time they are introduced to them. If people go into your site and don't find what they were looking for within seconds, they will click away and it is unlikely they will ever be back. So, you need to have a lead generation set-up on your website in order to capture your visitors' details from the first time they enter your site.

You want to be building your own list of prospects at all times and that means having a method of moving your leads from your social media and other online accounts you don't control into something like an email list that you own. This means collecting data, even just their email address so that you are then able to contact them with newsletters and other follow-up emails in order to nurture the new relationship you have with them.

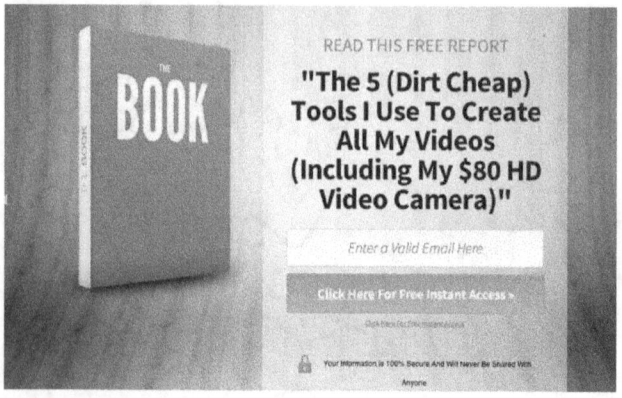

When we say lead generation, we are talking about setting up an opt-in form on your site, in which you request they provide you with their contact details in exchange for something that you are giving away free. What happens once you have captured those details is that your email system starts to send the subscriber a series of auto-responder emails and/or newsletters that will ultimately warm up that lead.

The auto-responders that are sent out should communicate a lot of value to the subscriber. For example giving away free gifts or opportunities or imparting some knowledge that will be useful to them and allow them to trial what you know and how you can help their situation specifically. This way you will build up your credibility and authority in your niche and develop rapport with your subscribers. The client is taken on a one-time journey with you that ultimately you want to end with them buying or engaging with your services. So that is the aim! Have your website set up in such a way that you entice the visitor to give you their details.

What Should You Give Away?

We often get asked the question; "what is the best thing to give away on my website?" In our view, provide something that delivers high-value and is a good example of what you do with the aim of giving its consumer a tangible result.

You want to give away your best content initially, not all of it, but just a good piece of it because you want to make a great first impression. The format of your giveaway should be based on your knowledge of your target audience and what that customer "avatar" would really like to see. For example, if your target audience is busy entrepreneurs, a great big e-book will probably not go down so well! Better options for the time-poor could include a podcast which they can easily download and listen to on the go, or a short "cheat sheet" which provides valuable information, but is quick and easy to consume.

That is not to say that e-books are now completely obsolete. There are some industries in which they will still go down well, especially if it is very niche and there is little competing information available. Again, it comes back to knowing your target audience and what it is they're looking for. What problem can you solve for them?

Here are some ideas of what you can create for your opt-in giveaway:

- **Digital Workbooks** - These are a great way to give your subscribers positive steps to take as they work their way through exercises or tasks which you outline in your workbook. Future emails in your funnel can deliver "keys" on how to engage with the workbooks or unlock points. Think of it as a treasure hunt where as people go through the first steps in your funnel, they proactively build upon what they learn until they have a completed "map" they can refer to again and again.

A great idea is to teach a process, with blank fields the user needs to fill out, so that when followed a specific result is achieved.

This is also a great tool you can use to upsell people into a webinar where you will guide them through the answers. Just make sure the workbook has enough value as is so people don't get an empty document where they feel they need to do all the work – they don't know you yet and don't want to jump through hoops to get value. Make sure it is transparent when they opt-in as to how they will get the value.

- **E-courses** – These can be delivered simply via emails with links to pages on your website or even in a member's only area on your website. The key with these courses is that each point or lesson still helps deliver a valuable result. You should not expect someone to go through the entire course to get a benefit (we are all busy after all). You want to deliver stand-alone value the whole way through. The bonus is that by monitoring which topics get the most engagement, you can gauge what your audience is especially interested in and even develop products specific to those topics.

- **Cheat-Sheets and Checklists –** Deliver valuable information in bite-sized chunks to busy audiences. You can share a personal rolodex of resources you know and use or a "map" or steps someone can follow to get a result.

- **Audio and Video Recordings** – This is a great way of "reverse engineering" content from an info product or membership site as teaser content. You can have it branded as part of a larger product to seed what else you have available. If you are launching a book, an audio version or a bonus video are a perfect way of building a list to then sell your book and add-on products or services to.

- **Quizzes or Surveys** - You've probably been enticed into a Buzzfeed quiz or two if you're a Facebook user. Quizzes conjure that curiosity factor among audiences, especially if your topic is juicy enough that they 'have' to know 'what type' they are or simply how much they know. There are tools out there which help you to build your own quiz and use it as an opt-in on your website. **TryInteract** is one of these, and it allows you to collect email addresses in return for giving quiz results. Just remember, you want your quiz to "stroke the ego" of the person doing it so they get a sense you will be telling them something good about themselves.

- **Physical Products** - This is not as common as the others because obviously physical products involve some kind of outlay of cash to start out with (don't forget shipping costs!). We've seen people give away USB sticks of recordings, or even free copies of their new book (usually for a limited amount of time). Check out sites such as Kabuki.com or Alibaba for ideas.

- **Discounts or Free Shipping** – Here's looking at you, ecommerce website owners! This can be relatively easily set up with tools such as **WooCommerce** on your WordPress website, or other ecommerce platforms such as Shopify. Create a promotion code that is emailed to people upon sign-up, and allows them to use it when they check-out with a purchase.

- **Free Trial** - If you have a member's-only website or online software or other business tools you can give away a free trial to access the content or use the tool. Don't underestimate the try before you buy model, especially if you are new to market and need to build a base of clients and case studies...

- **Free Consultation** – This will not be feasible for you if you expect a large number of sign-ups, but in smaller numbers, a free consultation provides a great demonstration of the service you provide, especially if you are a coach or consultant or in the B2B space. Think about what else you could offer as well so your prospect does not feel they are signing up for a sales pitch.

EMAIL SYSTEM TOOLS

MailChimp

The idea of using an email system is that you will be able to capture a list of prospects or clients and set up emails which will automatically be sent out to them – no more manually adding people to email lists!

One of our favorite tools which we usually recommend to anyone starting out is MailChimp. One of the cool things about it for beginners is that you can use a free version while you still have a relatively small list. This means that you can create your web form in MailChimp and insert it into your website for people to sign-up. Anyone who signs up is automatically added to a list of your choice and, at the same time you can have it automatically send out a 'welcome' email including things such as your free gift. As part of the free package, you will also be able to send out an email each week to your list, such as a newsletter.

Once you want to set up a series of auto-responders, this is where you will need to pay a monthly fee to use MailChimp. This starts at $10 per month which, let's face it, is cheap considering you can send up to 500 emails for that. They also have newsletter templates available so if you like, you can experiment with theirs before deciding to get your own designed.

One of the other cool features of Mailchimp is the various integrations it has with programs that you are probably already using in your business such as Paypal, Survey Monkey, Google Analytics, Twitter and Facebook, as well as many more.

AWeber

AWeber has been around for a while and starts at around $19 per month. There is no free version of this email service, however you can get a 30 day free trial to see how you like it. There are a few little extra tools available in AWeber but it really comes down to user preference in choosing a service. Some people prefer it because it has been around for a long time while others prefer the interface of Mailchimp. Both of these programs are able to automate your whole system from the basics you begin with, to your sales process or membership sites.

Active Campaign

Active Campaign sits nicely in between the first two programs and the next one. The difference is that it is set up as a database tool or CRM in the way that each person has one record and you have more flexibility to target them based on their behaviors taken with you.

That means it is easier to segment your lists based on your prospect's or client's actions taken with you. For example, if they buy a product you can automatically remove them from a lead funnel. MailChimp and AWeber use lists to store your contacts, whereas this one uses one record and then sets automation based on the behavior the person takes. This also means it can get more complex.

Ontraport

While we love MailChimp for beginners, we love Ontraport for those who have a larger list, are already monetizing their business online and want to start to look at full business and marketing automation as a next step.

Ontraport will cost around $USD297 per month, so why do we find it to be so good? MailChimp and AWeber are purely email programs; they let you collect basic data such as email addresses from your web forms along with some other integration options like payment forms. Ontraport is a full CRM system for automating your office essentials which also allows you to store full profiles for people. It also allows you to set up tasks to automate your customer service and alert your team to do things.

Basically, you are able to customize the data you collect; for example you may collect your client's birthdays, notes about them or products that they purchased. This means that you can store the entire history that each client has with your business and set up tasks or automated rules to support them better.

Additionally, Ontraport is linked up with a number of different payment gateways (PayPal etc.). This means that you can use sales forms through Ontraport and have payments process directly through it to your payment gateway. It will also recognize when your clients have bought something and store this against their profile.

Like the other two programs, Ontraport will also allow you to set up auto-responders and create web forms; however one of the extra-cool features of this system is that you can set up 'rules' within it. Active Campaign allows you to do the basics of this but nowhere near what is possible in Ontraport. For example, if someone has signed up to your opt-in form but hasn't clicked through on the link of your auto-responder email, you can set up a rule that sends them a reminder after a number of days which you choose. This is great because the system itself is recognizing whether you client is doing or not doing the things you would like them to and you can automate the whole process.

Another practical application of this is to segment your list. For example, you could segment based upon topic interests going by who clicked on which email. This makes it easier to be more targeted with your emails and send certain subjects based on the interests of the segment.

While this system will cost you a bit more, it certainly is top of the line in terms of functionality. Even if you start with one of the more basic email programs, you can easily export all of your data from that program to Ontraport later on if you wish.

The closest option to Ontraport, and another system that almost does the same thing, is **Infusionsoft**. We use Ontraport in our business and that is the reason why we chose to highlight it here. If you are ready for a more robust system then really it is up to your preference on which of these you prefer.

LANDING PAGES

One of the most popular posts on our blog is "What Is A Landing Page?" (Check it out: http://autopilotyourbusiness.com/what-is-a-landing-page/). This is perhaps because most website owners are realizing the value of bringing these into their marketing mix. Landing pages are where people "land" on your website and are designed to direct them to take a specific action that you want them to take with you – such as signing up for your opt-in or buying a product or service.

With your email marketing system, you generate opt-in form code which will sit on the landing page to gather the prospect's details. Now, there is an entire online marketing art dedicated to how to create the perfect landing page, but there are some tools available for you to use which allow you to choose from templates that have already been tried and tested.

Here are a couple you can try:

LeadPages

This is a favorite of ours which we use often. LeadPages offers a range of different landing page templates which they have spent time testing and analyzing. You can choose templates based on what your landing page's purpose is, for example webinar templates, video sales pages or the 'basic' squeeze page, or just pick one that looks suited to your purpose and modify it.

One of the cool, unique features offered by LeadPages is that you can sort the templates by the current conversion rates of all of their customer's pages, meaning the ones that have converted the best show first.

They also have a LeadBoxes feature which we use often on our blog posts – this allows you to have an opt-in button on a page, which if people click, will pop up an opt-in box. We use it to give away PDF versions of our blog posts.

LeadPages is a subscription service for which you pay a monthly or an annual subscription. They don't lock you into any contracts and you can cancel at any time.

Instapage

Instapage also has a huge library of templates, but you can't sort by conversion. However it allows you a bit more flexibility for design than LeadPages. It also has a great plugin for your WordPress website (just like LeadPages) which allows you to use your own website domain for your URL.

ONLINE MARKETING FUNNEL

With an email system, landing page and opt-in giveaway in place, you are in a good position to create what is known as a 'marketing funnel' for your business. The aim of a funnel is that it takes a customer on a journey with you, hopefully towards purchasing what you have on offer. The idea is that a funnel can offer prospects or customers suitable solutions at different levels of the journey, from the free giveaway for those who are investigating their options, to a paid product, and even on to a more premium offering.

The beauty of a well-crafted funnel is that the whole thing can be set on autopilot. From initial opt-in the customer can receive your emails so that they get to know you, and if they take actions such as purchasing, you can use some of the more advanced email tools for segmenting and refining how you communicate with different groups.

As an example, let's look at a possible funnel progression that a coach may use:

To start with, a prospect hits their landing page and signs up to receive their giveaway. From there they go into a series of autoresponder emails as well as the coach's newsletter, in order to help them get to know the coach better. Along the journey they could be offered a progression like this: low-cost product (a book for example), membership to the coach's membership website, group coaching, 1:1 coaching then a premium offer such as a retreat or mastermind. This way 1:1 coaching is no longer the coach's only option, freeing up a bit more time!

The structure of this funnel helps to solve the problem of being able to offer something of value to those who can't afford 1:1 coaching, while generating business for the coach. There is also a clear upsell path and defined segments, making the creation of suitable content much simpler.

Of course, there are a number of moving parts to a marketing funnel, with various landing pages, thank you pages and emails involved. You could build the whole thing yourself using email and landing page tools we've already mentioned, or you could opt to use a software platform that has been designed to build out entire funnels for you...

ClickFunnels

ClickFunnels allows you to choose a funnel by type (for example webinar, opt-in page, sales funnel etc.), and it will build out all the funnel steps for you. Once you have chosen a funnel type, you can choose page templates and customization options for the pages. You can even set up your automated emails from within their system, or ClickFunnels integrates with most major email systems.

If you use a shopping cart platform, they integrate with payment platforms too. They have also left it open to other integrations by allowing you to paste in HTML code (or get someone to do that for you if you're not sure!).

Testing and monitoring is an important part of any online marketing effort – ClickFunnels provides you with the tools to split-test and monitor your analytics throughout your funnel.

An advantage to using a tool like this is that it has everything in one place and is a great system for the typical small business owner who does not have a team of designers, writers and programmers to help. They have different levels of subscription unlocking different features or limits on what you can build, but they also allow you to have a 14 day free trial to start with.

In the end, it will come down to your personal preference. You may find that you prefer the pages that are available through the other software platforms, or you may just like having an all-in-one system!

TEXT MARKETING

Phone texting or SMS has increasingly become a more important marketing tool, as most people these days are carrying around a mobile phone.

It is a great way of sending out reminders and special personalized invites and discounts, and many CRM systems already integrate with an SMS system. What a lot of people are now doing at networking events is handing out a card and requesting that people text their name to a number on the card. That serves as a way of capturing data and opting the person into your list via their phone number. This means you can quickly and easily build a list and can start building relationships with the people on that list.

In this next section, we look at some tools and tips for Text Marketing…

Tips For Better Text Marketing

- Build your list of contacts the right way – that is by only texting people who have opted-in to receive text updates from you. In our experience (and that of other marketers out there), bought lists or texts to those who have not voluntarily opted in tend to only result in an "unsubscribe".

- As with email, try segmenting by interests. That way you can send texts only to those who have already expressed an interest in the subject. If you have a larger list, this will save you some money on the text numbers too!

- Keep it short and to the point. People want to be able to immediately see what's in it for them. Try and stick to the 160 characters or less which come with standard plans.

- Think about timing. There are two aspects to this – one is that timed offers tend to have higher uptake than anything open-ended, secondly is that you need to pay attention to the time that your messages are sent out. Test which days and times generate the best results for you.

- Don't be a spammer! The quickest way to lose subscribers is to bombard customers with texts of little value to them. Deliver value and only text when you really have something to say…

Now, let's look at some tools that are available…

Burst SMS

This is an SMS company in Australia that allows you to market via phone texting. You can easily upload spreadsheets of mobile numbers and create different lists and text messages from within your account to go out ASAP or to be scheduled at a future date and time.

Text Local

This is the UK version for anyone who is based there. Its features are similar to those of Burst SMS in Australia.

Instant Customer

This is a US based text marketing company which integrates some really cool features into their product. For example, it will send people messages back if they ask a question. Users can also scan or take a photo of a business card and it will automatically add those details to the database.

Ideas For Using Phone Texting

If you have decided on a phone texting provider and are thinking about the kinds of ways you can use this for your marketing, there are a couple of ways which we really like;

1.   Local Businesses

If you are a local business (for example a hairdressing salon), you can use SMS messaging to connect with clients if you have an upcoming special or competition. For example, try a message like "the first ten people to call this number get a free haircut". Friendly little texts like that also remind the client that you are around and keep your business in their minds if they are looking for your particular service.

2.   Events

If you ever run events or speaking engagements, SMS messaging is a great way to keep engagement up with attendees before the event. Often people are enthusiastic when they sign up but as time goes by, things come up and perhaps they forget or they start to make excuses as to why they can't attend. SMS is a great way to remind them and to say things like "looking forward to seeing you there". It's a great way to stay in touch with clients and rekindle their passion for attending.

3.   Competitions

A number of companies use SMS marketing for competitions, even advertising on TV. You don't have to spend big bucks for TV, instead your advertisement could be on print or online media.

Whether you decide that SMS marketing is for you or not, the time has come where mobile is overtaking desktop technology. There is a huge market out there for anything mobile-generated so there are many opportunities if you choose to take them up. Additionally, those who carry mobile phones tend to keep them very close and more people are likely to open and check every text message rather than open emails.

If you have been reading through these chapters and feeling slightly overwhelmed about the number of options available and what you should do, we understand! There are a lot of possibilities open to you but what we would suggest is to take one thing we have talked about that you can see is the right thing for you and start by implementing that. You can easily add other areas as you go.

6. SALES TOOLS

How do you process sales in your business? If you sell products online, but still need to be present for the sale to happen, then automation can help you! Alternatively, if you're not yet selling online but would like to be, then the tools we are about to show you will hopefully demonstrate how easy it can be to sell online.

Having the right system set-up in the first place will allow you to not only process sales, but capture analytics and store data on your customers too. In looking for tools to recommend our goal was simplification – they should be relatively easy for you to set up and use.

PAYMENT AND SHOPPING CART SOLUTIONS

PayPal

While there are a number of competing payment platforms that we could also mention, PayPal has become a mainstay of online marketers and remote workers worldwide.

We recommend it to the relatively new online business who is not keen to pay fees to larger sales platforms when they are not making enough sales yet to justify the expense.

Your PayPal account is free, but you will have to pay fees for transactions that go through. This is where the importance of scale comes in – most of the more expensive sales platforms are a subscription fee and you don't pay for each individual transaction. You will need to do the calculations for your business to see which works out better.

Paypal also will integrate with other programs that you may be using such as MailChimp, and it allows you to send and accept payments worldwide.

As a business owner, you may find that you hire virtual staff such as assistants, writers or developers – PayPal is a commonly accepted form of payment amongst the virtual workforce. You can also send and receive invoices, as well as access some basic reporting features.

If you only sell one or two products on your website, then you don't really need a shopping cart. You can use PayPal "buy now" buttons on your sales page instead.

There are other solutions out there like **Stripe** and **Braintree** which are great alternatives to PayPal. In addition there are full payment gateways like **eWAY** or **Authorize.net**, so it is worth looking around once you start bringing in a good amount to see if you can save on transaction fees.

Shopify or Volusion

Shopify and Volusion are all-in-one ecommerce solutions that will allow you to create a professional-looking store quickly, on their own platform using their templates, on your website. From there you can offer products with all kinds of variations, such as sizes, colors or personalization's, or showcase multiple views of products. You can easily link them to a payment solution like PayPal.

WooCommerce

This is one of our favorites for WordPress websites; WooCommerce is a free ecommerce tool that will allow you to create an online store and shopping cart for your website. It is downloaded as a WordPress plugin, and you can configure it to sell anything, including variations of size, color etc.

WooCommerce automatically integrates with PayPal, or you can download the extension specific to your particular payment gateway. It allows for configuring of tax settings and inventory management.

One of the cool features of WooCommerce is that there are a whole lot of extensions available for it that provide different functionality. Many of these you will have to pay for, but they make doing business so easy! For example, you could choose an extension for configuring shipping costs, or you could run promotions with coupon codes. You can add on an eCourse module or a membership area. You could set up an affiliate center for other's to promote your products.

Since it is a plugin for WordPress this means you have more control of how you set it up and the design, and of course you own the shopping cart rather then "renting" space on someone else's platform, like Shopify for example. However, with more options to customize there are potentially added levels of complexity to set up.

Mobile Payments

If you have the type of business where you need to accept payments on the go, or even offer different solutions in-store, then mobile payments might be something for you to consider. If you have that added option, it might even help attract new customers who would otherwise pass by, especially if you think of places such as markets where the customer may be put off by a "cash only" rule.

There are new mobile payment solutions being offered all the time, but here are a few to look at:

- **Square** – this service has been around for a while and is a good solution for those who need to accept occasional card payments, but don't want a merchant account. Square doesn't have monthly fees, but they charge 2.75% per transaction.

- **PayPal Here** – PayPal's mobile solution is a little different in that customers don't need to have a credit or debit card – they can also pay using their existing PayPal account. You can even charge straight from an app on your phone. If you have a normal PayPal business account you can apply.

- **Dwolla** - this is different again! There are no cards, readers or additional pieces of hardware involved as the whole thing is run on an app. Customers go into their Dwolla app and pay from a list of approved vendors. You can monitor in real time from your own mobile device. Fees are 25 cents per transaction, so this is a cheaper option.

Check also for mobile payment solutions that are specific to your own country – we found more than 30 out there! Your own bank may offer a mobile payment option, but check on what makes the most sense in terms of fees versus number of transactions that you expect to process...

FULFILLMENT SOLUTIONS

If you sell any kind of goods online that require shipping, then using a robust fulfillment solution will not only save you a whole lot of time, but potentially a bunch of storage space used in warehousing stock. The added bonus is that an automated system where a fulfillment house is quickly taking care of your orders should be more efficient and keep your customers happy!

Information Products

Do you have audio recordings, video recordings or written material that you'd like to physically produce and ship? These fulfillment houses can help, from the time of the order, to creating a high-quality product, to shipping it to the customer...

- **Kunaki –** this fulfillment house will create retail-quality products from recordings or designs that you provide on their website. They will include a case and wrapping on your CDs, DVDs or thumb drives and will ship straight to the customer.

As all products are produced on a 'made-to-order' basis, there is no need for warehousing of stock.

- **Corporate Disk Company (Disk.com)** – this is another option for your information products. They specialize in one stop full package production of CDs, DVDs, Printing, Packaging, and integrated fulfillment. Check them out for a number of creative ideas that are slightly different, such as silk-screening, glass mastering or molding…

- **CreateSpace** – This Amazon-owned company provides a solution for getting your book out, both in print and on Kindle. You sign up for a free account and upload your books and book covers following their guidelines. Books are produced on a made-to-order basis meaning that there is no cost outlay or warehousing for you to worry about. You receive royalties for any books sold, but of course CreateSpace keeps some as their payment.

Other Physical Goods

There are a large number of automated fulfillment services out there who will take care of every kind of product, even ice cream! Naming all of them would fill up an entire book, but here are some options to look at:

- **Promofill** - Automated order flow begins when an approved order is received from your shopping cart, customer service or inbound call centers. Every order is usually inspected by a member of a Quality Control Team to ensure the accuracy of each order. Most systems are scalable to handle 50 to 150,000 orders per month with the ability to manage multi-channel distribution.

- **Fulfillment By Amazon** – This is a pay-as-you-go service where Amazon will pick, pack and ship your orders. Their warehousing is available in the USA, Canada and Europe. You pay for the storage space you use and only for orders fulfilled. They will also allow you to fulfill orders from multiple channels from your stock at their fulfillment center. Unlike some other fulfillment solutions, Amazon does not integrate with popular ecommerce sites such as eBay or Shopify. This means that they don't receive automatic notification of orders from those platforms, however they have the advantage if you're selling on

Amazon. They will also handle customer service for your clients.

- **Shipwire** – This service has warehousing available in Canada, England, China, Australia and the USA. They are a little pricier than some other options, however they do integrate with popular ecommerce platforms such as Volusion, Shopify and eBay. Unlike Amazon, they do not handle customer service, so you would have to find another way of dealing with queries, complaints or returns (we've got some ideas coming up!).

- **Fulfillment.com** – This service has warehousing available in the USA, Canada or Scotland. They come highly rated by a large number of ecommerce business owners for offering a high level of service, but a cheaper price tag than many other options. Integrations with popular ecommerce platforms are available.

As we mentioned, there are a huge number of options when it comes to automating the fulfillment of your orders. The options mentioned are some of the bigger companies who offer solutions to small businesses, but check out any who may be local to you as well.

A factor to bear in mind is your cost of shipping inventory to a warehouse. The further away that warehouse is, the more it will cost you. Amazon has an easy process where you can request to send a shipment of inventory via your client dashboard, but most other options have a more complicated process where you need to arrange all shipping yourself.

You should also think about the level of service each are prepared to offer, and how much work or attention to details that they can take off your hands. For example, if barcoding is required, will they do it for you?

The ideal sales solutions will be those which free you from as many details of the process as possible. That's what automation is all about!

7. CUSTOMER SERVICE SOLUTIONS

There's been a little bit of stigma around automated customer service solutions, largely due to a reputation for being "robotic" or irritating (toll-free government operated phone lines, anyone?). It's fair to say that your reputation is on the line with every interaction a customer has with your business, so it's understandable that you want to be able to give top service!

As a small business, paying for staff and possibly office space to house them can be a massive undertaking. The overheads for things like rent, utilities and insurance can very quickly eat into your bottom line, so if you would like to be able to provide 24/7 customer service in an online world which never sleeps, you need a better solution.

HELP DESKS

There are a few options for 24/7 helpdesks out there, all of which run online, so that you don't have to be available yourself or have an office of support staff on hand.

These online services tend to run on variations of a monthly subscription model, with different levels available depending on the level of service your business needs.

The main idea of all of them is to provide support ticket management and to provide a quick response to your customers, so that they are assured that something is being done when they contact you. Agents are able to handle many enquiries themselves, but at the very least, where something needs escalating they will get back to the customer and let them know their query has been forwarded.

You can use a virtual help desk as part of your main "contact us" section on your website, but many companies are also having good successes by making help available when a customer has gone through to a check-out page. Having someone available to answer any last minute questions can help to reduce shopping cart abandonment, especially if the customer is leaving because they are unsure about something. If you've ever seen a little pop-up come up for 'live chat', then this is one of these help desk services in action.

As mentioned, there are a few different online providers to choose from, but here are three options that we like:

- **Zendesk**
- **Rhino Support**
- **Help Scout**

There are new ones popping up as well, including **Intercom.io** that are becoming more and more intelligent as to how they handle customer requests. Shop around to see what will best suit you, but one thing we love about these three is that they all offer a reasonable free trial period (30 days for Zendesk and 15 for Rhino Support and Help Scout). This should give you a good idea of whether they will work for you!

If you're still worried about the "robotic" factor, the great thing about these helpdesk services is that even though some use automated messages, an actual person needs to reply to your clients (no automated menus!), and they give you that added layer of professionalism for providing prompt service.

LIVE CHAT

There are other live chat options out there that will allow you to provide 24/7 support to your website visitors. We use **Zopim** on our websites. We love that you can hook it up with Zendesk and that you can customize how it looks. They also provide you with a decent analytics function.

Like most functions online, there are a few different options you can choose. Apart from Zopim, check out **Olark Live Chat**, **LiveChat Inc**, **Livezilla** or **AliveChat**.

VIRTUAL ASSISTANTS (VAs)

If you only get a few customer queries, or if you would like help with more than just customer service, then hiring a virtual assistant could be a good option for you.

Like virtual help desks, an advantage to your business of hiring a virtual assistant is that you reduce overheads. You can even hire in different time zones to support global clients, or to take advantage of differences in currency and standard pay rates. Your virtual assistant will get to know your business very well, and good ones can often have their responsibilities expanded as they go.

There are some possible disadvantages to hiring a virtual assistant that you need to be aware of, including:
- The risk that they are just not cut out for the job. You don't always know exactly who you're getting when you hire online, so we recommend getting references first.
- You tend to get what you pay for! You can't expect to pay bottom dollar for top-notch service.
- When communicating across time zones or even across different cultural backgrounds, there can be a lot of room for

misunderstandings. This is where we recommend having good systems in place to communicate, and ensuring that you clearly state what you want.

We have some great virtual assistants, and one of the things we love about them is that they also help to ensure we get things done that are needed! Managing our calendars and workflows are important jobs for keeping the business running and ensuring that tasks happen on time for clients. It definitely helps having someone else with oversight when things get really busy!

A good VA can help to create more seamless experiences for your clients, the key is to have robust systems in place (such as those we discussed earlier using tools like Process St), so that expectations are down in black and white. Vague instructions or expecting your VA to be a mind reader will rarely produce good results…

If you're wondering exactly what you would get a VA to do, here are a few tasks that they can typically manage along with customer service related tasks:

- Schedule meetings internally and with clients.
- Manage your calendar.
- Book travel and accommodation.
- Arrange details such as catering or printing for events.
- Pay bills.
- Remind you of important tasks.
- Help with spreadsheets, presentations or other software applications (depending on experience).
- Respond to or escalate customer enquiries.

Of course, many are open to learning new skills so the chances are you can outsource other tasks.

There are new avenues springing up online all the time to find virtual assistants and other remote workers, but here are a few to check out:

- **Zirtual** – If having a U.S. based VA is important to you, then Zirtual is the place to find them. They offer only VAs who are based in the U.S. and have met their minimum standards to qualify.

- **Virtual Angel Hub** – The team at Virtual Angel Hub take care of recruiting and training VAs for your business, saving you the training time and also help to train you in systems and delegation. They primarily service business owners in Australia.

- **Elance** – Along with the many other remote workers available on this site, you will find VAs from all over the world and with varying levels of ability and experience.

FAQs

Do you find yourself answering the same questions repeatedly from clients? If so, you can easily take yourself out of the equation by preparing good website content which answers those common questions.

The FAQ page is a simple, yet often over-looked solution. Simply compile a list of those common questions and answer them on the page. If you run a WordPress website, there are some great plugins to help you create your FAQs and to help your visitors sort or suggest them.

Here are a couple of plugins to check out:
- **Instant Q & A**
- **Templatic**
- **Sugar FAQs**

Along with your FAQ page, use your blog content to answer common questions that have some complexity. This is another good way of knowing that you're creating content your audience wants to see!

Make sure to build up your knowledgebase in your help desk as you go. This can be a helpful way of using searchable and sortable FAQs once you outgrow about 10-20 questions listed on a web page.

APPOINTMENT SCHEDULING

If you've ever experienced having to go backwards and forwards via email or phone to nail down an appointment, you will immediately see the value of tools that will do it for you!

You can transform the scheduling of meetings and appointments from another time-sucker, to a sleek process by using an online scheduler. Most of them work in a similar way – you offer options on the calendar for times when you are free and the client or team member selects what works for them. These tools will also follow up with reminder emails. If for whatever reason, the attendee needs to cancel or postpone the meeting, they can manage that through the link with the scheduling tool.

Our favorite is **ScheduleOnce**. It connects with the calendar you are already using (such as Outlook or Google Calendar) and integrates with other software programs such as Infusionsoft or GoToMeeting. It automatically converts time to the location of the viewer and keeps your calendar private. If you're trying to schedule a group meeting, you invite attendees who choose from times that work for them. ScheduleOnce will then provide you with the common times so you can choose a meeting time that works for all.

Here are some other tools, apart from ScheduleOnce that are worth checking out for scheduling:

- **Calendly** – Appointment attendees are taken to a page with options for times where they select and add their name. This integrates with Google Calendar, iCal or Outlook and has a base plan that is free.

- **Bookeo –** This tool comes in different types of editions for different businesses. It also includes marketing and payment options if needed. Bookeo includes a free option for solo practitioners.

- **Sign Up Genius -** This is a free (base plan) tool which comes highly recommended by people such as teachers or non-profits, who need to organize volunteers. You can easily create sign-up sheets for activities and include organizing who brings what and who runs which activity. Businesses have been using it to manage trainings and facility use too.

- **TimeTrade** – Another platform that offers online appointment scheduling and responsive engagement solutions for small to enterprise level companies.

The thing to keep in mind here is that if you schedule calls with clients, prospects or team members, or even create content for podcasts and videos where you need to set up interviews, then you will enjoy how these platforms can streamline this process.

If you can't track, you can't improve, so hopefully this chapter got you thinking about how to better track and manage your customer service so your customer feels supported by you and your prospects know they will be in good hands should they buy.

8. TOOLS TO MANAGE YOUR FINANCES

If tax time tends to be a mess for you (and your accountant!), then it's probably worth investigating some of the tools which make managing your finances more painless.

Let's face it, unless you absolutely love accounting, this is often an area of pain and procrastination for businesses, especially if you're still using more manual accounting methods.

If you're still writing in ledgers, manually producing invoices and stuffing receipts into shoeboxes, then there are some great tools available to save you time. The bonus is that you can also save your accountant's time, saving you money on billing!

ACCOUNTING TOOLS

Again, there are a huge number of tools out there and some will be specific to your country or region. Here are some of the better-known options that we like for small businesses…

FreshBooks – This cloud-based accounting software means that you can look after your business's books from anywhere. You can send invoices, track time and record expenses. It will allow you to accept credit card payments without any additional set up, create recurring invoices, send estimates and allow clients to view their history with you.

Even recording expenses is less of a chore – you can connect your bank account or credit card so that it uploads expenses, you can take a picture of a receipt and upload it to expenses, or you can manually enter expenses if you choose. Expenses are recorded in tax-friendly categories and all reports can be exported to your accountant at tax time.

Xero – Like FreshBooks, Xero is a cloud-based accounting program that will integrate with many other programs that you are probably already using. They provide a subscription-based service which comes with 24/7 customer support. One of the unique features of Xero that tends to out-perform other software providers is their multi-currency capabilities. This is only available on their premium plan at the moment, but if you are dealing in multiple currencies like so many global businesses now, they make it easy for you to record and convert currencies in real time so that you keep more accurate tax records! We are currently using Xero in our business.

17 Hats – This is another cloud-based program that could be described as an "all in one" tool, especially for solopreneurs or freelancers. The name should give you an idea – 17 Hats incorporates accounting, project, quote, email, calendar, lead capture, invoicing and contract functions to name just a few. The idea is that you don't have to run several different programs and can keep all of your business functions in the one hub.

GETTING RID OF PAPER…

Have you got receipts, business cards and other paper clutter stuffed in boxes, in the console of your car or lying around the house? There are some great apps available to help you de-clutter and organize those bits of paper.

Our favorite is **Shoeboxed.com**. They will scan your receipts for tax filing, produce expense reports, record mileage by tracking your mobile phone and even create contact lists from your piles of collected business cards.

Shoeboxed works with most popular accounting apps and is available on mobile or desktop. They allow you to choose how you use them – you can forward receipts from Gmail accounts, track using their mobile app, or stuff all of that paper clutter into a special envelope and send for them to organize.

QUOTES AND PROPOSALS

If you're still preparing documents in a word processing program for your quotes and proposals, there is an easier way! Quote software will help you to create a professional-looking proposal in just a few minutes.

Quote Roller is our favorite program for preparing our proposals. It has an easy drag and drop interface for efficiently creating your documents, and we especially love their analytics dashboard. This helps you to keep track of who is reading your proposals and which sections they are spending time on. You can even add interactive content such as videos.

If you have a team of staff who also prepare quotes, you can set up automated workflows, which mean that your team members can prepare documents, then automatically have them flagged for checking.

TIME TRACKING

There are plenty of good reasons to track how you spend your time, whether it's in order to bill clients or just to keep track of what takes up your time so you can see if you are doing projects that make sense for you to do or not.

MinuteDock is our favorite go-to for time tracking. Like most software programs, there are plenty of others to choose from, but we like MinuteDock for how simple it is to use and how easily it integrates into invoicing if needed.

They use "natural language" tracking where you can enter whatever it is that you're doing by just typing a sentence (Twitter style). As so many people see time tracking as a hideous chore, they have kept it simple so that you can categorize, shuffle and sort later.

You have options for how to track your time - MinuteDock is web-based so you can track with a browser window or using their mobile app. MinuteDock is tightly integrated with Xero, Freshbooks and QuickBooks Online (with Saasu and Freeagent on the way); meaning you can use your existing system to track and send your invoices.

With your finances, if you don't have easy-to-follow systems you can often be pressed for time just trying to work out if you have enough for tax, instead of proactively looking at your figures so you can get an accurate read of what is making (and losing) money in your company.

Try implementing a few of these ideas now. Your accountant will thank you for it!

9. TIME MANAGEMENT & TASK SIMPLIFICATION

There are other tools and tips which will save you time and simplify how you get tasks done, and these can have an even bigger impact to your business than the others we have shared so far.

This is because they help the scattered entrepreneur in you to stay more focused and keep you from getting bogged down in day to day minutiae. These tools have a big ripple effect when used, because they help you become a better leader to your team and a more impactful visionary, which will drive you forward when times get tough in your business.

COMMUNICATING INSTRUCTIONS

We've all got certain tasks in our businesses that we do repeatedly and need to communicate to others, or questions that we get asked over and over again. You can save yourself the extra emailing or Skype time if you have those FAQs saved somewhere with documented answers or can visually show what you mean in a quick video.

Many of the questions we get asked relate to how to use online programs. We like to create screen share videos or take screen shots of websites in order to make step-by-step instructions. We then store these on Basecamp, which is our central project management system or send them straight to someone via a link.

We use these with our team but also to illustrate clear instructions to clients on anything from how to place a Facebook ad to what to do on a new website we are building.

Here are some tools to check out:

- **Jing** – Create screen share videos (time limited) or take still screen shots. This tool is free and easy to use – you just need to install it on your computer. You can store your video on their server and then just send a link to someone to watch.

- **Screenflow** – This is paid software for Apple users which allows you to capture your screen and your camera at the same time. We also use this to create info products and even edit green screen videos. If you are a PC user then check out **Camtasia** for a similar tool.

- **Google Hangouts** – You've probably heard of live hangouts, but you can also use Google Hangouts to record instructional videos with no audience. You can easily share your screen to illustrate a point and use your webcam. The disadvantage over the downloaded programs is that you are relying on a good internet connection throughout your video.

AUTOMATING TASKS

While web apps have been created to make our lives easier, we can also find ourselves in a state of overwhelm trying to manage all of those apps and the ancillary tasks that go with them! Fortunately, you can apply automation to some extent if you use one of these tools:

- **Zapier** – This tool integrates with a vast range of apps that you already use (MailChimp, Dropbox, Gmail, Evernote, Twitter etc.). In fact, they have more than 400 possible apps to integrate with. This allows you to create rules that are triggered when certain activities happen within one of your connected apps. As a practical example (and one which we use), you might have Zapier send someone an email through Gmail when files are added to a certain folder in Dropbox. Or, you could create a rule where all photos which you post on Instagram are automatically uploaded to Dropbox.

- **IFTTT** – (If This Then That). This tool also allows you to set up rules that are triggered by events within integrated apps. It allows "if recipes" which are similar to the rules set in Zapier and "do recipes" which allow you to create your own buttons and bring in more "internet of things" technology, such as turning on lights or adjusting thermostats.

PROJECT MANAGEMENT

If you've ever had to spend a long time trying to find particular email messages, you will get that email is not the most efficient way to manage your projects!

Centralized project management software programs allow you to keep all of the information pertinent to each project organized in one place, as well as use them to set tasks and communicate with members of your team.

Here are some project management tools to look into:

- **Basecamp** – This is a cloud-based subscription service where you can create individual projects and invite the relevant team members to them. It is available on desktop and mobile and will track to-dos, allow you to assign tasks and let you know when tasks are overdue. You can upload any extra files that are needed to each project up to 10GB per file, so unless you have very large files, there is no need to have them stored all over the place.

- **Asana** – This program is free for teams of up to 15 people with the premise that "email is holding your team back". It allows you to set up projects and tasks, while keeping comments with each task instead of being scattered through email. While you could choose to stay on the free option, you do get a few more features such as private teams with the premium version.

- **Slack** – This is more of a communication platform, but you can easily separate conversations out to certain projects and you can also upload related links or files. Slack integrates with a whole lot of different programs, including Asana. You can add clients or team members to conversations, or keep them as private as you need. The platform has graduated subscription levels, starting at free but adding more features with each level.

- **Evernote** - This is a productivity app designed to help you "remember everything". Store files or things you've found there, invite others to share and create discussions on your work. Evernote also syncs with several other apps, such as Zapier, Smart Sheet and Scanner Pro.

SPEED UP DAILY TASKS

There are a whole raft of possible daily tasks that can be sped up or made more efficient with the use of a few clever tools. Saving a few minutes here and there can really add up throughout your day!

Here are a few tasks you can make more efficient:

- **Remembering passwords** – How many times have you spent several minutes trying to remember, then to reset forgotten passwords? Tools such as **1Password**, **LastPass** or **Roboform** have got your back. They securely store your passwords for each program that you use and autofill forms – no more remembering for you!

- **Writing** – If you're a two-fingered or slow typist, you'll appreciate this one – **Dragon Dictate** for Mac or **Dragon Naturally Speaking** for PC will take down your thoughts as you dictate.

- **Watching videos** – Whether you're watching a work-related video or getting caught up in YouTube (we know!), **MySpeed** is a great tool for speeding up the videos that you watch without you losing the clarity of speech or visuals. You can cut out a lot of watching time with it as there are always naturally pauses and other elements which lengthen video time. You are able to choose how much faster you would like to set it so that it suits your ability to keep up.

- **File Storage** – Apart from making sure your files are stored securely, using the right storage tool can also make collaboration more efficient. We prefer cloud-based solutions such as **Dropbox**, **OneDrive** or **Google Drive**. Never again do you have to worry that a broken hard-drive will cost you your work! Store it on the cloud, be able to access it from anywhere and invite others in your team to share and view your files.

TIME MANAGEMENT

What "time thieves" exist in your work day? You may be surprised to find out just how much time gets sucked away! The best place to start with managing your time is to know how it is spent and what can be done to use it more wisely.

Of course, you don't need to manually take notes – there are apps to help you track your time and understand what "time suckers" are in your day-to-day life.

Here are some you can try:

- **Rescue Time** – This time-tracking app will not only reveal your time-wasters and provide detailed reports, but will allow you to block those offending websites that take up your time for set periods (hello social media!).

- **Focus Booster** – If you are a notorious procrastinator or if you experience time-related anxiety, this is the app for you. It is based on the Pomodero technique, which advocates "sprints" to get tasks done and regular breaks in between.

We could go on and on, but right about now we have a feeling you are sold on automation! We want to make sure you start to action what you have learned and have a few inspiring stories to share so you can see the profound impact using these tools has had for other business owners.

You never know, you may get some great ideas for your own business!

10. CASE STUDIES

Are you ready to put everything together? We would imagine you are feeling overwhelmed, excited or both. The best way to understand something is to see how others have used it to create results for themselves.

Many very busy and influential people have managed to put systems in place that have ultimately helped them to be more efficient and successful.

We are going to share some examples with you of our real-life clients and we hope you don't mind if we refer to them by profession instead of name. After all, we don't want to give away too many of their secrets.

Case Study 1: The Speaker

One client who is a well-known speaker and does many events would usually gather a lot of business cards while networking with the attendees. Or he would ask people to contact him and put his details on the screen at the front of the room. Either way it would involve a manual way of following up.

Usually when the event was over he would go home and put all of those cards he had gathered into a bowl or drawer as he was just too overwhelmed to do anything further with them.

Or he would get emails from those who contacted him from the details on his presentation and would do his best to get back to them. However they would all want different things…some wanted calls, some wanted his slides, some wanted to talk about hiring him for his services and wanted to talk about which was right for them.

In his old system he was basically throwing away a lot of potential leads from people who were interested to know more about him.

He was growing his brand and was starting to get more speaking gigs and needed a new way of doing things, or else his speaking gigs were not really bringing him business…which is the exact reason why he was doing it in the first place.

He set up 2 landing pages:

He bought a domain and had it redirect to a ScheduleOnce booking page so people could go there and book in free time on his calendar and get the automated follow-ups the system sends out for him.

He used LeadPages to set up a landing page using another URL where he sent people to get his slides and any other bonuses and be entered into a follow up funnel that provided other great content from his talk.

He was able to use this over and over again. Now at the end of his talks he says; "Hey, if you are interested in taking the next steps you can book in a session with me by going here or if you want my slides go here."

There were of course still people that gave him their business cards, but this time he passed them to his VA (by taking a photo of the card) and she would enter them into his landing page for him so they would also get the slides and follow-up emails.

Case Study 2: The Lawyer

We have another client, a lawyer, who used to have the typical brochure website with a contact page. The prospects would have to download information and the lawyer never knew who was interested in her services.

She had heard that the best way to reach clients was to educate them on what you can do first with content. She set out to do a podcast where new potential clients could download her tips whenever they want and sign up for her newsletter to get updated when a new episode was released.

She was both building a list and also allowing people to get to know her in their own time. She also put a call to action at the end of her podcasts to send them to a page on her website to book in a free consulting session using ScheduleOnce!

She started getting new prospects by doing nothing more than creating podcasts and promoting them to her new list and on social media using Hootsuite.

Case Study 3: The Recruiter

One of our clients had a special situation where he had to automate 2 funnels…1 for the businesses who were his clients and 1 for the prospects he wanted to attract for the businesses to hire.

He also ran events where both sides could meet. He used to have a brochure website and keep a spreadsheet where he booked people into his events by putting their names on his spreadsheet and then emailing them with Outlook with more info about the event!

Now he uses automated bookings on his website for his events, 2 different lead funnels to warm up prospects with a podcast and videos and even assessments to prequalify candidates all run from his website on autopilot.

Now he is thinking of how to roll out his systems to other areas because of all the free time he now has.

Case Study 4: The Financial Planner

A Financial Planner recently did a big deal with an Accountant. The Accountant wanted to send his entire database over to the Planner to get specialized advice but wanted to ensure that his referrals would be taken care of.

They automated the introduction process via a membership site with great education resources. The Planner was given access to the new list of leads to email them logins to their new member's area. The Accountant recorded a welcome video that was used on the member's home page to make the new prospects feel at home with a friendly introduction to the Planner.

They now even produce educational events to these prospects and others every quarter and have put the entire booking process on autopilot using a landing page and automated follow-up emails and text messages to keep people informed about the event.

Case Study 5: The Stylist

When the stylist came to us she was looking for a way to both train other stylists and also build up her own practice. She also heard of the power of sharing educational resources so she ended up putting together a member's area where she had 2 levels – one for each type of client. She was able to add more content into the site and categorize who saw what based on assigning permissions to each web page.

If you were a style client you would log in and see style ideas and affiliate links to buy products and if you were a stylist looking to grow your business you would log in and see tutorials with upsells to "unlock" other areas of the site by purchasing more premium content.

Since the system was automated, it would send new members logins and upgrade them to different access levels based on what they purchased. She was able to focus on building traffic and let her systems do the rest of the work for her.

Case Study 6: The Chiropractor

This guy ran his practice by having a phone number on his website and a receptionist to take calls. He never thought about automating taking appointments on his website or even scaling his practice using his website.

Now when someone goes to his site they book in an appointment and are upsold into a membership where they can see him for an unlimited amount of times per year for a set price, which is promoting what he believes in...preventative health care.

Through this new system he also offers a member's only area of his website where he can release content to his new tribe easily by putting it on a private web page and emailing his members to have a look. Plus he set up rules in his CRM to email him and the member if they are not logging into the website and can ask them via a poll what they want to see more or less of. The alerts he gets allows him to personally follow up if he wants.

He now has a subscription based business that upsells new bookings into a membership and renews current ones all on autopilot!

....

Hopefully you got some ideas from these case studies about how you might start using automated elements in your business. The best place to start is whenever you find you are repeating yourself more than once to a team member, or you have to repeat the same thing to different clients. "Ding, ding" the bells go off...here's an opportunity to automate!

You are now armed with the tools to stop wasting your time...

...by repeating yourself, or making it difficult for prospects and clients to book in times to talk to you, or chasing proposals, or ensuring your receipts get accounted for (even if you stuff them in a shoebox), or following up with prospects, or remembering when to post something on your Facebook page.

Now we're off to the beach! ;) What about you?

WE LIVE AND BREATHE THE MARKETING AUTOMATION MAZE AND WANT TO GIVE YOU OUR SHORTCUTS...

We have helped over 10,000 business owners worldwide use automation to remove themselves from doing the things they can't stand doing in their businesses.

When you are able to let go of the tasks that wear you down, you suddenly have a business you love (and one that makes you money on autopilot)!

Here is where to GO NOW to get our latest findings: aybguide.com

We share things like:

- How we have tripled our traffic to our website
- Our favorite email auto-responder scripts
- Free trial access to our Digital Traffic Institute online community

We welcome you to join a community of business owners fed up with being a slave to their business!

www.ingramcontent.com/pod-product-compliance
Lightning Source LLC
Chambersburg PA
CBHW070933180526
45168CB00003B/1061